MY

POEMS,

SOUL

SHORT STORIES,

STIRS

JOURNALING

EMILY HOWE

CLAY BRIDGES
PRESS

My Soul Stirs: Poems, Short Stories, Journaling

Published by Clay Bridges Press in Houston, TX
www.ClayBridgesPress.com

ISBN: 978-1-68488-189-5
eISBN: 978-1-68488-176-5

Special Sales: Most Clay Bridges titles are available in special quantity discounts. Custom imprinting or excerpting can also be done to fit special needs. Contact Clay Bridges at Info@ClayBridgesPress.com

To Mike, Our Kids, My Mom and Friends

for always supporting my

BIG IDEAS

My life is the inspiration for many of my poems. I begin all of my poems with where I am, and then they start to take shape.

The layout of my book comes from a deeply rooted place in my heart. On the left you will find my poems, and on the right a brief description of my inspiration.

For example, "Curious" was born through the push-pull of the internal struggle within myself.

A lotus flower represents opening up. The lettuce represents being deeply rooted and growing through faith and love.

Enjoy the journaling pages after each poem.
Use these pages to put yourself and your own life experiences on paper.

Where does the poem take you? Journaling can be a powerful style of expression.

BATTLE

This morning on my mat
I am warm
I am ready
And I am present

My Breath
My Strength
The stories, twitches, music
Our Opener

Not long
It will go quick
Too sick
His time

The Color
The Stories
The Belly Laughs
Our lives

The Dancing
The embracing
And I am Present
For the Opening Battle

TABLE OF CONTENTS

GOD ROCKS

This morning on my mat
I feel cold
My heart is warm
And I Rock
Yeah, You Do!

I hear the hum
The breath of my Husband,
In the distance my kids
And They Rock

My Head is Heavy
My Heart is Heavy
She is in the distance
And She Rocks

Her heart is Heavy
Her head is Heavy
And She Rocks

Their Pain
My pain
And She Rocks

Care to Share…
Here we Go…
And She Rocks

I lay on the Ground
Feel the Beat in my chest
And They Rock

Who likes Games?
I ponder on the Ground…
He loved Games

And the MAN Upstairs
I Hope you know Who
Yes, GOD ROCKS!

"God Rocks" takes the reader through all the different important people in my life.

My husband and kids are mentioned first. Since we've had children, I find myself rocking when I take a moment to be still.

We are blessed to have several generous, loving people in our lives. "God Rocks" touches on several of those relationships.

Journaling Space:

BATTLE

This morning on my mat
I am warm
I am ready
And I am present

My Breath
My Strength
The stories, twitches, music
Our Opener

Not long
It will go quick
Too sick
His time

The Color
The Stories
The Belly Laughs
Our lives

The Dancing
The embracing
And I am Present
For the Opening Battle

Life's struggles are mentioned in "Battle."
I am always working at feeling and being present.
I'm finding out that when I grieve, opening up is helpful to work through my emotions.
In December of this year, it will be three years since my Dad passed.
Recently, my father-in-law received news that his long battle with cancer had taken a turn to Stage Four.
This poem ends with remembering my Dad's Celebration of Life.
I was very present, and was strong enough to give his eulogy. My Dad was a wonderful storyteller. He told great, colorful jokes as well. We danced to happy, upbeat music that day as we remembered my Father.

Journaling Space:

THE LIGHT

This morning on my mat
It is cold
I feel light
She is light

My light is dim
I stay on the ground
I feel a pull

My ears are open
My eyes are open
My light flickers

Time for steady
Rise to balance
Shift my gaze

I see the brick
I feel the wall
And I'm standing tall

My strength
My power
My light is bright

This poem begins on my yoga mat. It was written in my head during class. This was one of my first days back to class and back to moving. For a few days I just stayed low with my movements, not coming up to stand at all. The patience of my yoga teachers allowed me to move and stand when I was ready. I found my balance and used points on the brick walls to steady myself to get back to my inner strength.

Journaling Space:

THRIVING

Today I am in the driver's seat
I'm clear
I'm steady
I'm balanced

I stand tall
I pick a spot
My fingertips brush the wall
Balance comes with my breath

I feel my feet on the ground
My breath in my chest
I fidget, I shift
Balance finds me

The spot is clear
My toes claw in
My hands and gaze rise
And I Thrive

While driving after early morning yoga, this poem was written in my head. Being in the driver's seat also means I was in complete control and felt great on my mat.

Journaling Space:

VIVID

Sitting in a shop
My thoughts
My memories
So crisp in my mind

The toys in the sand
I hear the wind
I feel the cool air
I'm home

The bell rings
We run to the line
The cage is broken open
The laughter begins

We meet again
We begin our journey
Our hands reach out
The Rings bind us

The cries and tears
The dimples the toes
The blessings are plenty
It feels slow but moves fast

Here we are
And I am still
My chest tightens
My thoughts are Vivid

In this poem, I'm sitting in a coffee shop with friends reminiscing on our childhood together. I was considered shy and alone "in my sandbox." In 5th grade, the cage was "broken open," representing my humor and my storytelling. Then, the poem leads to marriage and starting our family.

My Memories, big or small good or bad, I remember them vividly.

Journaling Space:

SIGNS

I'm sitting up today
There is a light
It doesn't flicker
Is this a sign?

Tradition has importance to us
The light is on
The light is off
He messes with us

Expecting one thing
They are on their own
We wanted independence
We sigh

It's the one they remember
Is it Blue or Gray?
I know what they would say
The sign went up today

We follow, we love
We walk slow, we love
The Ray of light comes down
There are signs

This poem was written while driving home from seeing one of my Roots (a friend of four lifelong friends) in the play Fiddler on the Roof. It was excellent and made me think of my own family and their traditions. Ever since my father's passing, I have experienced many signs that I believe are small visits or ways his presence is made known. In "Signs," he is the flicker of the light in my car.

My expectations have gotten my hopes up one too many times in my life. All my husband and I ever wanted was for our children to grow up strong, healthy, and happy, while leading independent lives. Now they are doing exactly that, and as our nest empties I feel it daily.

Journaling Space:

ESSENCE

I lay in the dark
It's early morning
I hit the snooze
My heart beats fast

I'm far from home
But still unchanged
Today I will go
Like I did as a child

The beauty…
The grace…
The music…
The peace.

Pillars of strength
Statues of Saints
Notes from an organ
Touched by my friends

Blessed until next time
Sent out to our world
Dad was so sorry
Cleansed Essence

While on a recent trip to Boston, I attended Sunday morning mass with a friend we were traveling with. The beauty of this church was awesome. I lit a candle for Dad, which brought me peace and grace. The music was very familiar and took me back to memories of my Catholic Church growing up. This poem leads to the next entitled "Mercy" as we find our way back to Church.

Journaling Space:

MERCY

We walk the trail
The past repeats
He is so very merciful
He is so very good

We have been away for too long
We are finding our way back
He has been here the whole time
And I knew He was waiting

We shifted for convenience
Support was given at the time
Guilt came later
As we find our way back

I work through the pain
Not every day, the pain
But I always knew
He was waiting

Does it matter where?
Some would say no
One opinion matters
As we enter today

I Believe
I know
He shows
God has Mercy

Years ago, when we moved into the home the kids remember most, we switched to the neighborhood church for convenience. Years later, when the guilt and humiliation we experienced within that church became too much, we left abruptly. It took us three years to try and become members at a different church. I'm so happy we did. And I am confident He has mercy on us.

Journaling Space:

STILL

As I kneel on my mat
I think of the fun
The full weekend we had
Friends near and far

The park and it's past
The monster
The friends
The memories

The Ducks
The sounds all around
The drive
The high five

The Game is Fast
The Bear wants Noise
The arena is Loud
And It is Sweet

We seek the quiet
Back to the Noise
The wind is chill
The water is still

A fun, fast, full weekend of volleyball, baseball, breakfast, and friends and family all wrapped into about forty-eight hours.

Journaling Space:

GRANDIOSE

As I drive
I think of my dreams
Always big
Still big

Their dreams
Their journey
My journey
I slow as I remember

I feel the anticipation
I think of the meeting to come
So happy I have his support
Over 30 years, actually
Forever and always

Look forward
Look down the path
Are my dreams big?
I know they are

And I don't care
Who knows it
They are not
Grandiose

After a recent diagnosis, the word "grandiose" has had a negative effect on me. My poems were already underway, and the dream of publishing a book was born.

Journaling Space:

REVELRY

I sit in the sun
Remembering the stories
The laughing
The crying

Big families
Many celebrations
Highlights for sure
Holidays are plenty

Gatherings slow
They slow
The pace is different
There was glitter

Shining in the yellow
The memories calm me
Loved our time
It closes quick

Some blame him
No blame
No wrongs
Revelry

My husband and I each come from large families. We are used to entertaining and having gatherings at our homes. We have recently downsized our home, and as the family continues to age, we are not meeting as often for our traditional celebrations.

Journaling Space:

GROUNDED

I sit up today
I breathe today
I'm grateful for today
I dig in

Hands and Feet
I claw in
Blocks assist
Balance wavers

Dreamy kind of day
Eleven is the time
What will they say
What will he ask

Exciting stuff
I can't hold in
Friends know
She knows

I Bound out
I Bound back in
Meant to be
I am grounded

This poem begins on my yoga mat, then references getting the appointment with Lucid Publishing scheduled for 11:00 AM in a few weeks. I had just started writing after our recent move. It hadn't even been a month. I was so excited, but I knew my husband would have lots of questions since publishing a book was so new to us. I told a few friends, and I told my Mom. I was excited but also confident in my work and creativity.

Journaling Space:

SUCCESS

I stand tall on my mat
I look over at him
So very proud of us
Full of Pride

He is our traveler
Searching for roots
Humor so humorous
We can't deny him

She is our caregiver
Stayed close
Connects often
Loves much

Passionate steps in
The roar of the crowd
A bleacher beneath us
The face of a champ

It's time for some adventure
He never sits still
Some may say the favorite
We say he's chill

The joy we see
Our love is real
The Pride we feel
Their Success

I mention each of our children in their own stanza. This poem brings me to talk about their personality traits and lives. It ends with us full of joy and pride in our children's current journeys and our confidence in their success.

Journaling Space:

TRANQUILITY

I sit up in bed
It's early morning
Work is humming
The heat has started

The sky is black
Dark black tonight
Colors could be found
Behind a lens

Awake alone
Takes me back
Bottles and diapers
My four precious babies

All grown now
The need not so great
The feeling when they do
Helpful and kind

We each provide
Moments of Grace
This night brings
Tranquility

On this particular evening, the Northern Lights could be seen. Tranquility then leads to the middle of the night or early morning hours. This time often brings me back to when the kids were little, and the need was great. As they grow, the need is still there, just not as often, and not for a diaper change, or a warm bottle. Last night they needed a signature, grocery money, and help with insurance questions.

Journaling Space:

ADAPT

I sit and breathe
Feet on the ground
Breath in my chest
Weight in my shoulders

He's not far
They aren't far
I feel far
And I wait

The plane begins to climb
The lights are dim
The bumps are there
And I breathe

Searching for ways
Easing my mind
Breathing is slow
And the plane is high

My head begins to settle
He helps with a smile
I breathe deep
And I Adapt

On a recent flight, as we climb, I think of my family I will soon return to. The weather shakes me, but my faith carries me through the air. My husband smiles from across the aisle, and I adapt.

Journaling Space:

DECADES

As I lay in bed
I think of the shops
The food and drink
My Friends and Angels

The signs
The windows
The displays
I take it all in

Our generational friends
From near and far
For a decade to date
We Nourish our souls

Spring or Fall
We come from all
To take in the tours
Oh the laughter and tears

Through these years
We have made bonds
Bonds that last into
Winter and summer

Now to pack,
Will I get it all in?
We are ready for…
Decades

My husband and I have been part of a NHBA (National Home Builders Association) Builder group for over ten years. The "Seekers" have made many lifelong friendships.. I look forward to these trips during the fall and spring every year. "Decades" represents these friendships, and our group recently celebrating ten years together.

Journaling Space:

PEACE

I sit in the waiting room
I ponder the moment
It takes me back
When my littles were small

The rocking I've done
The child I've seen
The young Mother I spoke to
The Mother that spoke to me

The community is small
I see an old friend
We speak of the past
We remember it well

We talk about what's coming
The pumpkins and treats
We reminisce and
Our name is called

I'm startled a bit
I stand up quick
I follow my son
And I am at Peace

Our youngest son and I are in a doctor's office waiting room. I see a young mother with her son. I began to chat with her as other moms did for me when we were their age. I immediately felt a connection to her and remembered the many trips to the doctor when the kids were younger.

Journaling Space:

DECISION

As I sit in the car wash
Decide on my day
Indecision sets in
While I'm in town

I live in the country now
A town, some would say
Some might say
She didn't like the city

Some would be wrong
I love the hustle
We love the hustle
Thrive in the noise

Find Peace
In my heart
In my small town
In which We live

Do I miss the city?
Partly we would say
They might say one thing
And us another

We decide together
It is what we do
No indecision…
As we make Our Decision

Downsizing and getting down to basics and the simple life is on my mind after a recent move to a smaller home. After seeing a smaller car on the used lot on my way into the carwash, I made the decision to talk with Mike. Sometimes this is how fast I make decisions. This led me to recall what others in town were saying about our quick move. Decision-making can be challenging in a marriage, or any relationship, but we make them together.

Journaling Space:

BREADCRUMBS

I sit on the couch
Look out into the dark
The early morning sky
As they sleep I wait…

As the years go by
We learn to share
We still care
As each drops crumbs

When I sit by myself
It is quiet
I'm not quiet
I drop crumbs

My family is near and far
We will gather together soon
Oh the fun we will have
As the crumbs continue to fall

The quiet will fade
The volume will raise
The smiles as I gaze
See the crumbs?

We laugh, we joke, we cry
Some may be inspired
Some may be confused …
With all of these Breadcrumbs

"Breadcrumbs" was written just before Thanksgiving. Through chatting with one of my cousins regarding aging parents, aging ourselves, and the dynamics of having a very large family, she spoke about dropping breadcrumbs. Little hints just enough for someone to know, but maybe not enough for everyone to know what is being discussed. Gathering around the table with a large family, the volume will go up. The loudness has been missed greatly, and I look forward to my time with my family always.

Journaling Space:

GREAT

Soon I will sit in the stands
The stands of champions
Some come today
And many came before

Outside now statues
These Greats Used to be In
Now up on a tall green wall
Names and Dates in gold

The parking lot fills
It's a noon game today
Come early, they said
A breakfast for Graebs'

Our friends of old and some are new
They sometimes stir, we are strong
Since 5th Grade not always Great
Now we stand together outside The Greats

But before the Gate
One of my favorite parts
We let things cool
And we go inside and be Great

We find our number on our seats
Feel the roar of the crowd and the crisp air
We get cozy, and snuggle in…
The tunnel opens…Here come the Greats

This was written prior to a tailgate party before a Packer's game. Lambeau Field is a pretty cool place to watch a football game. Statues sit outside the stadium. Many names of past players are listed on the walls of the stadium. Being a team player has been important to us to instill in our children. The greats can mean many things, however; in the above poem, they refer to the players on the field.

Journaling Space:

SCAM

I sit in the car
The Noise is up
Clocks fell back
Back to Central

The wind blows
It's powerful today
The leaves move across the grass
The wind is strong

The truth or just noise
Bots or bods
Smart phones Bruce?
Our first born

The trends the words
LouLou sets me straight
I Thank her often
But do I care?

Fraud at the game
She buys the magazine
She doesn't get the shoes
He missed the Ad…

The noise fades
I breathe deep
It's a New Day…
That's not a Scam

The day after a busy weekend. This word was given to me by a friend's daughter who had experienced a fraudulent business transaction. I had also just experienced fraud on one of our personal credit cards. These issues inspired this poem, along with my phone still thinking my firstborn's name is Bruce instead of Bryce. Smartphones sometimes make me chuckle. Even though, they help us so very often, even as I write in this book and talk to text.

Journaling Space:

DIAGNOSIS

As I lay in bed
I ponder what's to come
How will others react?
Extended versus Immediate

Small communities are a blessing
Some may stay inside
I have opened
Self-diagnosis versus actual

Denial versus admitting
All have something
We look inside
Will we see it?

Stages vs types
Four or Two
One a sentence
The other gives Hope

Choices to make
Our time is a blessing
Careful as it runs out
Type two is the diagnosis

So often, we are put in different boxes. Different diagnoses can happen throughout someone's life, or people will tell them what their issue may be. Will they accept that? Will they look for help for that, or will they deny it? I have recently dealt with this in my own life, and diagnoses can be scary.

Journaling Space:

HOLDING

As I lay I reminisce
I've held them all
Still do from time to time
One more to go

The baby, they say
The favorite of mine?
Standing on
All the same

I find myself
Trying to
Hold on tight
He's slipping away

Independent they say
What we wanted
Of course
Why wouldn't we

Not far away
Very close now
No penalty here
Still Holding

Holding on tight makes me think of Jacob… this last year of having him home as a kid. He will be eighteen and a High school graduate soon.

Our relationship has grown so much in the last few years. He's becoming a nice young man, and I love spending time with him. He's funny, caring, and can be a stinker at times, but he's ours.

Journaling Space:

IMPRESSIVE

In my favorite spot
I'm wrapped in a cozy blanket
It's game day
I settle in

I think of the season
Her last season
The leader
She has become

The friend
The mentor
The player
She has become

We are waiting
We are packed
Leaving soon
This Team is Ready

They've Trained
Worked
Steadied
Practiced

This team is Ready
These Coaches are Ready
Together they are
Impressive

I wrote this poem on a recent trip to watch our youngest daughter, Kate, and her college volleyball team. I think of the team and her, along with their coaches, and watching them grow as a team. They were all ready to bring home the W.

Journaling Space:

STRETCH

They stand near the curb
Pick a Bus…
Comfort found
Their hearts filled

Filled with
Nerves
Anticipation
And Grit

First in Years
Ten to be exact
Updates in Cases
And Banners

The Bus fills with
Music
Laughter
Heart

They've arrived
Dress for Game Time
They begin to…
Stretch

Kate, our youngest daughter, recently made it to nationals with her college volleyball team. This poem takes you through their bus ride down to nationals. Knowing these girls, it was full of music with a little laughter sprinkled in.

Journaling Space:

TODAY

In the early morning, I sit
It's bright out
I'm wide awake
I settle in

Being in the moment
Present tense
Here and now
The clocks are ticking

My stomach is growling
The refrigerator running
The ice shifts
The water fills

I feel the soft chair
It holds me
The blanket cuddles me
I feel at home

I see pictures from the past
A plant growing in the distance
Snow covers the grass
I am safe and loved Today

Being present in the moment has been my focus for the last few years. Looking back on my children's childhood, I wonder if I was really present. It's a question I ponder often. I am very mindful now and appreciate all of our blessings, especially the gift of time with loved ones. As I edit this book I am now confident I was present. Just the other day I looked at a painting of a beach scene. This painting brought me back to taking the kids to the beach, and the memories came back vividly.

Journaling Space:

PASSIONATE

Sitting up in bed
Our work ethic started young
It runs deep with us
I would say with all of us

He is Strong
Families Future
Calm and Steady Goals
Work Dreams to come

His is Strong
Future gets closer
Goals stretch out
Dreams are His

Hers is Strong
Future is Hers
Goals are in sight
Dreams are just right

Hers is Strong
Future in Structure
Goals of inspiring
Dreams of Business

His is Strong
Future in large equipment
Goals to work hard
Dreams are simple

It runs deep with us
We Jam and we Party
We pause to Focus
We are Passionate

This poem is about my husband and our kids and how we are all passionate in our own ways, and the strong work ethic Mike and I have instilled in them. I think of our family's passions for all different things and their characteristics.

Journaling Space:

AVOIDANCE

Sitting reminds me
Of when this word
Came to my mind
So many times in my life

When things get hard
Scary
Close
To home

I stop in my tracks
I think
I run
Repeat

Why
When I know
They have my back
He has my back

Excitement builds
I got this
This time I won't let in…
Avoidance

Avoidance has started to set in with my most recent idea of writing this book. It's not as easy as when I started. However, I know I have a lot of support at home and through my strong faith, I will see this project to completion.

Journaling Space:

FAIR

Sitting up in bed
An ever changing world
Or word
Or is it?

Old Habits
New trends
Short while
History repeats

Old Friends
New ones
For awhile
History repeats

Old ways or New
Trophy or Trophies
Tradition beats on
History repeats

Our world
Our time
Does it have to feel…
Fair

This poem is about raising our children to know life isn't always fair. Giving them life lessons from our old school mentality. We grew up when only the winner getting a trophy or a prize. The poem then takes a turn towards friendships that may not always work out, and usually for the better. God has a plan, and our faith sees us through.

Journaling Space:

DIRECTION

Passenger seat
I type
My thumb sometimes
Can't keep up

Thoughts are reeling
Building a Reel
Reel spins
Connection sucks

Construction ahead
Quickest way ahead
Is it?
We shall see

Home is where
Headed today
Heavy
But PROUD

All ways…
Are His.
We sometimes take
A different direction

I wrote this poem on the way home from a recent trip out of state with the kids. I took a ton of pictures and was putting a reel together to share with friends and family. While we were in the car, the connection was spotty. I am proud of all our kids every day, and the different directions they take.

Journaling Space:

TRANSFORMATION

Sitting in my seat
Road trips keep us going
Falls can be tough
Set to get through

First
Working Always
Happy seems settled
He's creating

Second
Works Often
It's not a race
She's Caring

Third
Plays Hard
It's been Tough
She's Leading

Fourth
Plays Harder
On our Toes
He's Driving

We are proud
Most from Him Above
Touch of us Here
Proud of Their Transformation

When the kids were small we started a Road Trip tradition over their holiday break. "Transformation" is about our kids as they continue their separate journeys, all with their own personality traits.

Journaling Space:

QUIET

I sit in silence
Mornings bring tasks
I hear the rumble
Silence is broken

Anticipation closes in
My heart beats loudly
Silence on my mind
Time to work

My mind surges ahead
Back to the noise
We thrive
They thrive

The buzzer sounds
Regionals done
Sparks We are
Court or Stands

Now to the car
We dance and sing
Our exit in the distance
Soon back to the Quiet

Prior to leaving for Madison for my daughter Kate's volleyball tournament, I got some work in. Her final volleyball season had us doing many midweek road trips to support her and her team. On the long drive home, we used music and dancing to stay awake as we celebrated another win.

Journaling Space:

REPLENISH

Church is in sight
This writing in my mind
Get it out
There's a fire

Tend to it
Set her free
She is stronger
Inside

Tend to it
Let her be
She is still
Inside

Tend to it
Bet on her
She is balanced
Inside

Time to regroup
Time to nourish
Time to feed
Replenish

"Replenish" takes me back to my internal struggle of looking to God for strength. Through my faith, I am stronger in my stillness and more balanced inside. Our visit to church always helps recharge our batteries for the week to come.

Journaling Space:

NOW

Sitting in a comfy chair
I open
No more closures
I'm Being

Out then in
Deep breaths are taken
Others are taken
And I breathe

Soon the vitals
will come
Needed for strength
Wanted for healing

I wait for the change
Halfway there
I sit very still
Back to the Grind

On the way out
Noise in my head
That echoed through the room
Loud and clear Now!

"Now" records my struggles with a recent Type 2 Bipolar Disorder diagnosis. Struggles with mental health are a very real thing for many people, and I pushed it away long enough. I've been in this waiting room before. This time is different, I'm ready now.

Journaling Space:

SOUL

I sit in my car
Outside the Waves
Back three days now
Not my body

I've been away
I'm slower
I move differently
No one notices ❤

As I drive away
The anticipation of fun
My breathing slows
My throat tightens

I have missed them
Some have been away
Some have been close
I love my friendships

Not my body
God's Body
I'm ready to go
Firing up my soul

My Soul is so very comfortable on a yoga mat. So much so that when I'm away and then return I may not do all of the poses, or I may move differently than the class, but I'm okay with that, as are my teachers and classmates. It is a completely judgement-free zone. We are truly all there for ourselves. After yoga, I go to coffee with friends, which fires up my Soul.

Journaling Space:

PERCENTAGE

I’m in the passenger seat
The sun beats in
Feeling like a 6
He goes Fast

Not last year
That was almost 3
8 months was given
There’s time

We have time
Use the time
Be in the time
Love the time

Stop the push
Let it go
Stay now
We got this

Let me finish
I’m not done
He’s not done
Part of 94…is my Percentage

I wrote this poem three years after my father passed away. "Percentage" takes me through all the percentages of recent diagnoses. We will take the eight months we have been given. We will use, and feel, and be present in the time given. Only God knows this, it is His plan, and it is time to stop pushing and just be. The poem ends with the percentage of my own Bipolar Type 2 diagnosis.

Journaling Space:

CRIPES

Driving up the hill
Soon to go down
It's a warm fall day
One of the last they say

The road is windy
I drift
I noticed the bumper
The bumper says Christ.

I think to myself
So I ask…
Siri goes to France crêpes
Smart they say, sometimes maybe

Heading to a friend's
Many leaves are down now
The fall is coming to an end
Winter is close

Local girl
And I'm at peace
Who cares what they say
Cripes!

Cripes is a Midwest slang term used with humor in mind. Literally, while driving, I noticed a bumper sticker that I believed said Christ. This is how fast a poem can come together for me. I turned to Siri for help. I say "Cripes," and Siri turned French in a heartbeat and came back with the word crêpes. I had a good laugh.

Journaling Space:

NOTES

In the dark on a bench
I hear beautiful rhythms
The beats move me
Music plays

Just the music
Keys being struck
Then the words come
And Cords are sung

I'm taken back
We are in the parlor
But this time no tune
She strikes them anyway

I don't hear the difference
He would hear it
Maybe they did hear it
Maybe they saw us

Gone too soon from us
Music was encouraged
Still is strong with us
As we sit playing Notes

A lifelong friend recently put my poem "Breadcrumbs" to music. On a recent visit to her childhood home, we sat at the grand piano in their formal living room. We couldn't find a light, so we sat in the dark with only the flashlight from my phone shining on the keys. She began to play and sing. Music was always a part of their home. I was not bothered by the out-of-tune piano. Our fathers, who are both deceased, maybe heard us that night playing the notes.

Journaling Space:

ANTICIPATION

Passenger again…
My chest tightens
What's next
Who knows

Pages perhaps
Bindings perhaps
Numbers perhaps
Nobody knows

Time to start the race
We meet and Breathe
We want it
They want it

Time to get up
Time to go in
Your turn baby girl
Let's Go!!!

She is Passionate
They are Passionate
We are Passionate
Anticipation…

I was anticipating many things as my husband and I thought of a possible book deal. Pages, bindings, numbers. I will race towards anything that I'm passionate about. Kate is passionate, and our kids are passionate in their own lives. Mike and I are passionate about our big ideas and plans, too.

Journaling Space:

SURRENDER

I nestle into my mat
It's a chilly morning
My mat warms fast
We move with intention

It's a Monday
The wind is blowing
Connecting is seamless
Concentration comes and goes

Quick trips and meetings
Friends in town
Family out
But very close

Games in future
Possible Game
We pass
In town Friends

Will They…
Will He…
Will I…
Surrender

I surrender to the pace of this life we love. The busy life that our family has created together for over thirty years now.

Journaling Space:

PRESENT

Waves of Morning Chill
She says Be Here
I feel it
He loves them

One Carrot
Two Potatoes
Diamonds
Newspaper

Comics a favorite
Favorite Holiday
Memories are all now
Three years now

She loves him
We love him
God opened up
For him

I work on me
Each day
Always Being Here
Present

My father loved Christmas and gift-giving. Being present can be difficult, but giving can be so fun and a chance for creativity. This will be our third Christmas without Dad, but the presents wrapped in newspaper continued, especially the comics, which were his favorite.

Journaling Space:

TIME

I sit at Mom's
Stool under foot
Clocks ticking
Head is heavy

Shoulders tight
We laugh together
We relax
And Enjoy

Tuesday's our day
Errands to run
A day off
We fill it up

She plays her game
As I write
We have today
We use today

Tomorrow not promised
We have today
We use today
Full of Time

"Time" takes me through the Tuesdays spent with my Mom. Mom's home is full of clocks, from chime clocks to cuckoo clocks. I appreciate all the time we have together, and love our Tuesdays.

Journaling Space:

SPLASH

We sit in the stands
We spread out
Get to know
Our surroundings

To my left, quiet
She takes in the day
Enjoys the sun
Enjoys the day

To my right
She takes in the day
With a lot to say
Asked to hold

She continues
Tries to enjoy
The right gets louder
Cans on the ground

Asked to slow
Starts to slow
About to leave
Then a Splash

This poem is about a recent Packer's game with friends in new seats. We get comfortable in our seats. My friend quietly takes in the day. The couple to my right got louder with every beer can that fell. Prior to looking over and noticing they left, an inappropriate story was shared, and there was a splash.

Journaling Space:

WORKING

I sit at my desk
Loving what I do
The sun shines in
The wind moves the trees, distant chimes

Love to feel needed
She coaches me
Love to give
I find my purpose

Love to feel still,
He prompts me,
loving the quiet
Love to feel

Love my balance
He gives to me
I find the ground
Love to feel at peace

He moves with me
I'm more still
Steady
They're working

I love my work and have found a purpose to look forward to. I'm enough, and work adds a little life back in. This poem not only runs through work, but also through the steps I've taken working with my life coach, my yoga instructors, my psychologist, and my psychiatrist.

Journaling Space:

MAGIC

I sit in the quiet
Except for the clocks
She helps at a meal
I wait to paint

It was a beautiful fall day
Leaves were swirling
She chimes
It's almost time

Time to get creative
He's very creative
Everything is temporary
I trust in him

She likes crafting
We go together
Favorite place to be
My Family

I don't know how he does it,
Santa every year
No matter where we are
It's Pure Magic

"Magic" starts by me sitting at my mom's, listening to the clocks again. I was waiting to paint with our oldest daughter, who is creative in her own way. Mike is also creative with the spaces and moves he has planned for us.

Journaling Space:

CURIOUS

I sit and I wait
Questions are asked
Some don't understand
I'm opening up

Many questions
Few answers
Many petals
I'm opening up

Lots of irons
Getting rid of some
Fewer irons
I'm opening up

Starting to understand
I don't care who
They are all that matter
I am opening up

Lettuce grows
Lotus flowers open
She says…
Stay Curious

Through working with my life coach, she has asked me to stay curious. My curiosity has helped me open up through my poetry. As I'm enjoying writing, I've stepped away and begun to delegate other tasks I was in charge of. Some people are starting to understand, others don't, and I don't care if they do. Writing helps me and fills me, which in turn helps my relationships.

Journaling Space:

INSPIRED

In my seat
Now they are tall
Remember them small?
We do

Continue to
Give Back
Want it
Take a bite

Continue to
Love Big
Want it
Take a bite

Continue to
Play Hard
Want it
Take a bite

Each and Everyday
You're Ours
We are
Inspired

"Inspired" mentions all the ways we have strived to raise our children. We are in the home stretch of having four independent, strong young adults. We are so very proud and inspired by them every day.

Journaling Space:

BREATHE

As I look out
I see the river is still
Lights to my right
Smoke rises up

Thankful for my breath
My strength
My heart
My courage

We are blessed
We are aware
We work hard
We pray harder

Try to be good
Try to be Caring
Try not to tire
He is good

He allows us
She asks me
We continue to
Breathe

I breathe and find my strength, heart, and courage. We are aware of how very blessed we are. We give back and look to our faith. God gives us our breath, and my life coach and yoga instructors remind and prompt me to use and find it.

Journaling Space:

DETAILS

Still on a drive
Music is pumping
Pumped for info
Memories as well

Doesn't always use it
Set your watch
Not by him
Loyal as Hell

Will he
Won't he
Can't ever say
Loyal as Hell

He likes surprises
Keeps us on our toes
Our Maverick
Loyal as Hell

Ping, Pong Blows up
Deets takes the lead
They named him.
He likes…Details

A childhood friend and I have become closer over the last few years. He loves details, needs details, thrives on details. Along with this, he is a very loyal friend.

Journaling Space:

HOME

As I sit in the driver's seat
I think of the plans
Boots in his future
For work with his hands

Mouse to us
Work to do yet
Stay strong kiddo
Until the end

The finish is coming
Fight the battle
You got this
Stay until the end

You may fly now
Reminders will come
Mouse
This is not our end

Always and forever
The heart
Remains and
Will be Home

Our youngest, Jacob, will graduate from high school in June of 2026. He will enter the trades field and will work with his hands like Mike. He has the grit and passion for it. He seems more settled in the things he loves faster than our older three. Being the youngest of four he has grown up fast.

Journaling Space:

SPRIG

Sitting on the bottom step
I feel the chilled floor
Just beyond the door
I took it all in

Yesterday in the sunlight
The stones and trees
Each could fit in my hand
These hands have tended four

The last tree
Brand new
Fresh from the ground
Will it make it through

It's colors caught my eye
I crouched down
I zoomed in
Will it survive the winter

This tiny starter
Will he grow to be mighty
Our colorful little
Sprig

The actual sprig of a colorful maple is pictured with my poem.

The sprig represents Jacob, our last born, the baby of the family. He is a senior in high school and will also be gone soon. He has big dreams, and we support them always.

Journaling Space:

WARRIOR

I sit in the sun
It's a crisp fall day
The door pops open
There are some flaws

Hearing the news
Brings me to look at the sky
There are wisps of white clouds
They move south

She is close to me
She is close to her
I see a stone
I washed it up

It has flaws
We are flawed
He is close
They embrace

Prayers to them
They are strong
She is strong
Warrior

"Warrior" takes the reader through a journey of a good friend finding out her sister was very sick. As I sat outside in the sun, I looked at the stones I was surrounded by. I found one and took it inside to wash it up. I drew a heart on the stone and sent this poem to my friend, who is a warrior like her sister.

Journaling Space:

CUP

For years
You knead it
Pinned as
Tradition

She slips a little
Gets an option
Several come
Stronger than ever

Quality
Got her back
Prayers are full
Stronger than ever

Pace set to zero.
Hell no…
She's a Rockstar…
Baby!

Powerful,
Knock on the wood
Others have tried
Her Cup

This poem was also inspired by a friend I see at weekly coffee who has been struggling lately. Over the years of seeing her at a local coffee shop, we have become friends. She has been a customer there so long that she has her very own coffee cup there.

Journaling Space:

LEAVES

As I drive to a friend's
Piled high
End of the roads
Many things coming to an end.

Seasons
Reasons
Cares
Life

Ending soon,
Hopefully not too soon
We will make it
through together

Decisions have been made
Now we wait
We wait for the fall
We add to our table.

We wait together.
Our favorite place to be
Celebrations are many.
We enjoy the Leaves.

During our recent season of fall this poem was inspired on a drive as I saw all of the leaf piles. For many, the fall of emotions can come in the fall and winter months as the days get shorter and darker. With the end of Fall, comes many celebrations with family. But first, we enjoy the leaves.

Journaling Space:

TWINS

Sitting in my spot
West Twin flows slow
Leaves float East
Running in the family

Running towards the dam
Summers are plenty
I gaze at old friends
She stops home quick

Prepare for a short trip
Dinner with dessert
My stomach expands
Twisting and turning

Great friends still
Miles between
Make the plans
Keep the plans

Peas in a pod
Feels like family
We could be…
Twins

Living on the West Twin river now brings the poem "Twins" to life. We prepare for an early dinner with Friends we see at least once a month. Friendships take work, and the ones that last are worth the work.

Journaling Space:

GAMBLE

Life can bring jokes
Surprises
Games
And fun

Life can bring stories
Long Tales
And sadness
No Drama Zone

Surprises aren't bad
Some can be good
I don't like surprises
Finding joy in Life

He was a jokester
He's a jokester
I'm a jokester
We tell silly stories

Roots are four
For the fun
No matter how long
Ends with a gamble

"Gamble" reminisces on friendships and drama-free zones. My best friend informs me that not all surprises are bad. This helps me find joy in the little things. I think of my Dad, Mike, and myself being the funny ones. Roots has been my group of friends since junior high school. We have over forty years of friendship between us.

Journaling Space:

CHECKS

As I sit on the ground
Sundays are key
Time to think
What comes this week

Yoga check-in
Monday morning check-in
Duck check-ins
Coffee check-ins

Yoga comes early
Starting
Moving
Breathing

Monday comes quick
How are you being
What are you seeing?
What are you doing?

Sunday already
Fun was had
Love was received
All these checks

All Sundays bring the weekly planning to me. Signing up for yoga for the week. Monday morning check-ins from my life coach, and Sundays take me through the Checks.

Journaling Space:

LOUD

I sit in the car
I've left abruptly
Majority gets us
Louder does not

I can be loud
For the right reason
I can be passionate
For the right reasons

The fuse is quick
Judgment sets in
Time to breathe
Find my balance

Caution sets in
Questions are asked
Truth is not given
But given to him

His opinion only
Matters to most
Seems like not all
Time to get Loud

During a recent confrontation, I chose to walk away instead of engaging in something that could have escalated. My fuse can sometimes be quick, but I use my skills of breath work to find my balance and to calm myself.

Journaling Space:

TIRAMISU

In the car
In her driveway
Check in with my love
Team meeting he said

Birthday boy
Survival is key
Family & Friends
Surround and support

West side of town
Double for a bit
Not for all
Downtown we go

Downtown
I was wrong
Wingys for days...
Love my town

Back at the meeting
Candles are needed
Will it hold up
Tiramisu

This poem is about a silly conversation between Mike and I at a recent celebration where a song came up, and we were debating the words.

Journaling Space:

TIRED

I sit up
It's early
Pitch black out
I think of the evening

Dinner at a new spot
We support
Small town restaurants
Will they support?

Next up
Live music
Visits with friends
Family pops in

Then to the Friday night haunt
Southwest End
The Usual
Music is played

Years later they still talk
Past emotions pop up fast
It ends in a hurry
So Tired

"Tired" starts with a dinner at a new restaurant in town. We will support as we have failed at a restaurant in our past. We then checked out some live music and ended at a family spot. We listen to the rumor mill and I am tired of it.

Journaling Space:

STAY

Resting in the sun
Preparing for winter
Which Shirley will come
We'll meet friends later

From the beginning
We have stayed true
So many things
Our one Love

Too many things
Keep us apart
Crazy at times
I'll say it again

Continue to thrive
Many many keys
One place to another
Communication

Our love is strong
Twenty-five plus
Some would say
Stay

"Stay" takes me through Mike and I's twenty-five plus years. Through my years away, we stayed true to one another. Many things come up to keep us apart, but we stick together through it all. Through all of the moves and adventures.

Journaling Space:

FAITH

In a pew
Sun shines through
Diamond Windows set high
We Be

Born
To them
In Faith
We Be

Perseverance
With Them
In Him
We Be

Settle in
Relax in it
Sleep will Come
We Be

Being can be difficult
He Provides
We Be
In Faith

After our last move, we have recently joined a new church. It is a beautiful building, and as Mike enjoys the architecture I watch from afar as he takes it all in. Born and raised Catholic, we have returned to the Catholic Church, and we follow our Faith.

Journaling Space:

SEVENTY

Sitting near a barge…Big blue waits
Water ways
Rivers
Canals

Long trip
Importance
Quiet but Important
Majestic

Slow
But long
Only way
Majestic

Many will watch
Park and enjoy
Celebrate
Majestic

Hidden Building
Rumor has it
She goes out Tuesday
Seventy

A recently built crane in our Home town of Manitowoc, Wisconsin, launched out of the Manitowoc River to Washington State. This was major news in our small town. This crane is Referred to as Big Blue, and the number 70 is stamped on the Crane.

Journaling Space:

FANTABULOUS

I reminisce as I type
Past Friend
The Laughter
Remembering the Fun

Country Days and Nights
Friends Near and Far
Oh the Fun
We all Had

I'm told I'm Funny
I'm Creative
A good speller
I'm Me

My choices
My decisions
My Friends
My Family

Slow your role
A bit much
Gifting feels
Fantabulous

A quite silly word from a friend but I ran with it. Near Christmas time, I get in the giving spirit. As I look at the now wrapped gifts, they may be right, but I love it!

Journaling Space:

MARSHMALLOW

Standing near the fire
Sun and fire on one side
Wind blows, I hear the crackle
We turn around

West Twin on the other
Ripples in the water
Trees line the river
My back feels the warmth

Hands in my pockets
Cold watch on his wrist
Bury my face in his chest
Feel the cold on my chin

The wind blows the flames close
The ash rises up
My eyes squint a bit
As I type my sweet poem

Turning and turning
Not dizzy
I feel like
A Marshmallow

Another poem to show my personality. We recently had a fire in the frigid winter in Wisconsin. At one point, as I spun to stay warm, I thought, "I'm like a marshmallow being toasted over a fire."

Journaling Space:

PITS

Life throws challenges
Tipped or spiked
Passed or slammed
They hit us hard

Shifts in position
Shifts in your thinking
Shifts in your prayer
Shifts you through

You come out as a
True mentor or friend
True partner or parent
True sister or brother

Stay strong
Head up
Look up,
He's got you

The challenges
Keep coming
Tossed or thrown
It can be the Pits

"Pits" focuses in on one's faith and belief in oneself. Pits takes you through life's struggles and how we persevere, truly showing our strength and how we can adjust and adapt.

Journaling Space:

REMAINS

On our ride into town
Morning begins
I see the crescent in the sky
I feel the warmth of my seat

I'm questioned
When I arrive
I settle in
To my warm mat

What is left
My favorites?
New favorites...
Not

I work
I think
I find it
Stronger

My Feelings
My strength
My power
Remains

Mike and I go early to work out each morning. On this particular morning, the moon was still up. Some of the moves in yoga are not my favorite. Once I let go and just be, I find my strength.

Journaling Space:

CHASE

I'm driving at night
Chasing my purpose
Chasing the pride
Wanting him to be proud

I'm proud
proud of him
proud of our children
proud of our family

Feeling like a kid again
wanting to get my way
Tears begin to fall
Something's getting in the way

Trust him
Trust me
Trust them
Trust in God

He has a plan
I have a plan
There's always a plan
Who loves the Chase?

After another lengthy discussion about my latest Big Idea of publishing a book, I drive home, and I'm following Mike. My Pride sets in, I'm so excited about this and want it so badly, I begin to cry. This poem describes my faith in Mike, myself, my children, and in God.

Journaling Space:

ANCHOR

I balance on my mat
My foot grounds me
Holds me in place
I touch down for a second

What else will
hold me,
or push me
Down to the ground?

I fight for Balance
Gravity will not win
It's a war right now
Peace in the end

Who else will
Hold me
Or push me…
I stand Tall

My Balance
My Breath
My God
My Anchor

Faith gets me through this yoga class, and I can find my balance against gravity. As I stand tall, I find my balance, breathe through it, and find my Anchor through my God.

Journaling Space:

LOSS

I lay in bed in the early morning
How many have gone
Too many
To count

Family both so young
We grieved but then
Too many
To count

Friends both so young
We aged and then
Too many
To count

Life has many things
We grieve throughout our…
school, jobs, church, sports, and
Our community

Through it all we learn to feel
Empathy, Resilience, Strength,
Courage, Compassion, and
We thrive despite our Loss

Our own personal experience of having a large family brings a lot of loss. We are also part of a large graduating class and have seen a lot of loss.

Journaling Space:

GAINS

Sitting and reflecting
A full and fun weekend
Reflections on the water
Peace in my heart

Where we live
A great history is known
Our Community's history
Plenty for All

Theaters and Museums
Gardens and Trails
Dunes and Beaches
Plenty for All

Jewels and Gems
East and West
On our lakeshore
Plenty for all

Some have never been, some go often
Support is given
Community owned
Not for profit have…Gains

Our small community has a rich history. A museum and a symphony orchestra are both celebrating 75th anniversaries this year. So many non-profits are lending a helping hand in our community.

Journaling Space:

TIES

I see ice has formed
There's a chill in the air
Trophies for days
History repeats

Faith
Since we were small
Ready for Church
We wear these

Work
Blue and white
Colors hold honor
We wear these

Equal
Flags billow
Stand in the wind
We wear these

He is constant
Purpose earned
All needed
Some wear Ties

"Ties" takes me through all of the collars that exist in our lives. We wear ties to church, perhaps, or at least our little boy did on his own one time. We wear different colors in the workplaces we choose. Colors of our flags that represent our countries, states, or clubs. God is our constant through all of this.

Journaling Space:

BEING

I sit as the TV is on
It's on but I'm not listening
Solid in our thinking
Level is difficult

I drift away
Strange how that can happen
So easy
Presence is tricky

The volume goes up
My attention
I'm caught
Presence is tricky

Pictures surround us
I glance in his direction
Phone in hand
Presence is tricky

We zone out
Focus comes
We lock eyes
Presence is Being

This poem was written about watching TV one evening. Drifting is easy for me at this point in my life. It's a challenge to be in the present moment. As the volume rises, I'm caught drifting again. As I glance in Mike's direction he doesn't seem to be present either. But then we lock eyes, and we are back.

Journaling Space:

STEMS

I'm slowed in the car
wandering and thinking
Past conversations and ideas
My mind goes to them

Habits are formed
Pulled from
And turns to
A Nail-biter

Life happens
Daily…
Hours, minutes, seconds
A Nail-biter

Release
Ease
Find it
A Nail-biter

Where is the pain
Where is the stress
Somewhere
It Stems

Stress shows itself in many ways, and can form habits. A friend gave me the word Nail-biter and the poem morphed into the name of "Stems." He tried to stump me, but I feel like he enjoyed the finished product.

Journaling Space:

PERCEPTION

We sit and enjoy
Reflect in the window
We are touched
However we're opposite

Sounds all around
Time to listen
Care to listen
Just listen

Opinions
Everyone has theirs
One matters
Just listen

Truth
Read to the end
Don't stop too soon
Just listen

Time to be complete
Pay attention
Stay in your lane
Perception

"Perception" focuses on communication and listening to ourselves, and the truth versus the lies that are out there. Sometimes I feel like you need to verify everything you hear or see these days.

Journaling Space:

FUNNY

As the Flakes Fall
And I talk to myself
I begin to giggle
Birthday Eve

Many years ago
The Shell was cracked
Crack myself up
Own best Customer

Years ago he said Yes
There was a Mall
An Outlet
Own best Customer

Soon a Party
Slip and Slide
Will We go
Own Best Customer

We will Visit
We will Laugh
We will Sing
I'm Funny

My sister-in-law gave me this word…

I went to my Roots with it. One of my dear friends (a Root) celebrates her 50th birthday tomorrow, as I write this on her Birthday Eve. My "Roots" is a group of friends, we have been great friends since Middle School.

Journaling Space:

PERSEVERANCE

I sit up in bed
I reach out
I wake up
I chuckle with him

Years ago there was a pause
Cancellations
Friendships strengthened
Time was plenty

Gratitude is shown
It's felt
It is given
Love

Gather
Enjoy laughter,
Stories,
And time together

An announcement is made…
Keep on keeping on,
Dirt has said.
Perseverance

Persevere through all the different things life throws your way. When there is time to give, then friendships bloom. Thanks is given, and laughter and stories are in full supply. Mike quotes the movie Joe Dirt, and we laugh together.

Journaling Space:

DREAM

It's early
Before the Sun
The light is dim
Not dim enough for some

Big weeks ahead
We get prepared
In all different ways
For different things

The Tasks will start to
Roll in, Trickle in
Check them off
One by one

Was this always the plan
The journey has many shifts,
Changes, bumps, and hiccups
We find our way

This one is recent
And new, it's mine
I am the dreamer
Of my dream

Thanksgiving has come and gone, a card is chosen; I am the dreamer of my dream. This poem was written in the car after yoga class, preparing for gathering around all the different tables.

Journaling Space:

COMPASS

Watching the flakes fall
Gazing to the East
Out at the West
Soon to drive South

This time of year
Friends go North
Others stay near
Now we wait

West to the center
Soon we will gather
Our party of 10
Love grows

Missing them
Excited to come together
Flying East, and South
Friends and Family

All these directions
All the Love and Joy
We feel it, we love it
Our Compass

Christmas and waiting bring the need for patience. As we wait for Jesus's birth, we practice this patience. As we wait to gather all together as a family. This is our first year of being a Party of 10. All our children have boyfriends and girlfriends now. Gathering and being together is our favorite place to be.

Journaling Space:

PEPPER

I'm bundled
Covered in white
Fresh and beautiful
It hugs the trees

A game to warm up
Or just to stay fresh
The pace is set
Start the match

Spice up your life
Or your dish to pass
Trust can feel
Like a game

Grows near the ground
Since we were small
She liked to play
We are a hit

Watching from above
Joking and laughing
As the time passes,
A word comes to mind…Pepper

My younger cousin, whom I used to babysit, gave me this funny little word. I think she was trying to stump me. I think I nailed it, if I do say so myself.

Journaling Space:

BACKWARDS

Teddy bear Sundae
Mouse laughs
Times spent there
Reminds me of

The place to go
After concerts, recitals,
Scouts and more
Special events

It's Sunday
He gets ready
Removal starts
Our Church

Beyond words
He is good
A special place
Always have loved

Towards the River
I see it's not solid
This poem is
Backwards

Once the first snowfall on the river was in the bright sun, it reminded me of a special ice cream shop in town. This place was visited during my childhood, and our children's childhood as well.

Journaling Space:

BURNING

The River begins to swirl
As the wind kicks up
He comes in
Cheeks have reddened

Full of Magic
Just appears
Love is deep
In our hearts

Packing not happening
No snowman
Just angels
All around

Later a fire
Will burn
Cleaning up
He is good

We believe
Coffee is fresh
Taste is
Burning

A large snowfall recently came to town. This stops several people in their tracks, but not us. Mike removes the snow, and I want to build a snowman; however, this time it's not packed snow. Angels are possible, and the thoughts of Santa and Christmas are closing in. Another great winter day for a fire!

Journaling Space:

LAUGHTER

As I'm leaving the State
I think of the Street
Work is light
With many hands

Gifted
Good intentions
We laugh
Wrong holiday, lady!

Fun to be together
Stories are told
Turns into joking
Laughs are plenty

We will gather
Bake and exchange
Celebrate our friendship
Around the table

Clever banter
Softballs are thrown
He makes the Bread
And the Laughter

"Laughter" comes to me from my sister-in-law. It takes me to all of the fun in our lives, and the laughter that comes from many. Prior to a recent trip to Hershey, Pennsylvania, I think of how we will be planning and working on our Christmas treats together.

Journaling Space:

INTRUDERS

I sit and think of my ideas
Who will support them
He's always been
By my side

Big or small
Standing close
Almost our lifetime
Stay

Feelings are strong
Weakness sets in
I lean in to the feelings
Unbreakable bonds

Few are not close
They don't know
Understandable
They are distant

My ideas are big
Along for the ride
They act like
Intruders

Back to thinking of my book, as the planning stage begins. Some will support me from the beginning, and some won't understand it at first, or ever. I don't care, and I'm not scared to keep them at a distance.

Journaling Space:

WHISPER

It's early morning
Lists of things
In the dark
I find my way

I try
My footsteps
My voice
Stay quiet

He's resting
He's gathering
Strength for the day
He's quiet

I head downstairs
Make my coffee
I sit, my mind
Begins to wander

Quiet my mind
Lower my voice
As I talk to myself
I whisper

Shortly after my recent diagnosis, and as I get older, the earlier I wake up. Waking up prior to the rest of the house can be challenging for me. Being quiet is a challenge for me. I love to talk, share, and tell stories.

Journaling Space:

LOVE

I sit across from him
Life keeps coming
We stay close
We roll with it

Beginnings
Good and bad
Too many to count
Endings

Loyalty
They struggle
Teach by example
They build Trust

Safety
In our arms
We try to shelter them
From Pain

Security
He calms us
I feel their
Love

This word comes from a friend. This one comes easily as I feel the love from him and them daily. We live through beginnings through loyalty. We have found our safety in each other. We give each other security, and our faith and love get us through.

Journaling Space:

HUNGER

Sitting back and I watch
Watch the changes
The time leaves
Too fast

Goals
Set them
Work at them
Be with them

Dreams
Dream them
Think on them
Stay with them

Starting
First steps
Jump in or Check in
Set Challenges

We have instilled it
Our kids have grown
They have their own
Hunger

"Hunger" speaks to our children and their goals that we encourage them to set, dreams we encourage them to have, and how the first steps can be taken towards them. Now it's up to them to run with it.

Journaling Space:

REJOICE

I reflect as I snuggle in
So many memories
They return in a blink
Like they never left

I can hear it already
The music will shift
Their volumes will raise
Our chests rise

He watches over
God is good
I'm not scared
I care

I can see it
Their smiles
Their movements
It's what I've missed

Meant to be
Not hidden
In our time together
We Rejoice

This poem entered my mind as I sat in church. I wrote it when I returned home and snuggled in. We are happy to be back in the Catholic church. As we were raised Catholic, we have missed the songs and the feelings that mass brings as we rejoice.

Journaling Space:

FOOTSTEPS

I look out the window
I see them one by one
On the bright white snow
It blankets the river

I follow them
Their path comes to an end
The kids' ending is nowhere near
So much life to live

Lead or follow
Whichever you choose
Remember, He's good
Look to Him

Guidance can be great
Lean into your faith
Think back
It has always been

We are here
He is here
As we see from a short distance
Your footsteps

After a recent fresh snowfall on the river, the morning brought footprints in the snow. I followed them through the window until they left my view. Faith and following God come to my thoughts for our children and family again.

Journaling Space:

WELCOME

As we enter in the dark
The floor squeaks
A touch of Christmas
We relax

A long day
Patience
Waiting
Wondering

In the quiet
I think of him
The mighty
And strong

As I wait
I practice
And enjoy the Wonders
Of Jesus

As we prepare
For Giving
And receiving
We are Welcome

On a recent trip to Hershey, Pennsylvania, the sign on the wall said, "Welcome," and there is today's word. There is A small Christmas tree in the corner. Also small touches in the kitchen of the upcoming Holiday. As we remain patient for the arrival of Jesus we feel Welcomed in our new surroundings.

Journaling Space:

CHOCOLATE

My feet are up
I peer into the kitchen
Magic happened there
Treats for days

Loved ones
Frozen for travel
So many shapes and sizes
Enjoying being present

Soups and breads
Preparing starts
Sampling begins
Catching up

Sweets
Brands compete
It's the sweetest
They are too

It's in the air
Time together fills us
I breathe the sweet
Chocolate

A few states away, we gather with co-workers who have become friends. We are so very happy to be here with them. As we gather to make our treats, we share soup, bread, and stories as we catch up.

Journaling Space:

SLOWING

I Sit at my desk and notice the snowfall
Some are fast
Some are slow
Up late today

Running fast
Left to right
Through the things
All the things

Falling slow
Like today
Noticing more
All of it

Week filled fast
I was asked
I said yes
Here for all of it

Is this the fall?
Is it coming?
So many questions
Am I slowing?

This poem takes me through seasonal depression and being curious if this was me needing a rest, or if the bottom was going to fall out again. Would I stop? Would productivity leave me again? I've struggled to find my purpose. I work through that to this day. My faith and my yoga practice help me stay grounded. And I will continue to work at it daily, not only for me but also for my family and friends.

Journaling Space:

MEMORY

I look past the twinkling lights
Out to the cold
So beautiful
And so cold

No snowmen
No forts
No angels
Just thoughts now

To when they were small
Bundling up
From head to toe
Fun for them, a break for me

Peeked out
Wrapping up
Heading in to warm up
Start to prep the Hot Chocolate

Snowmen, forts, and angels
Building Togetherness
Laughter and smiles
What a memory

I'm very curious of what's to come as our nest empties. Memories have been flooding me as the seasons of fall and winter have forced us to slow a bit. This memory is from a snowy day when the kids would get bundled up and run out to play. It didn't matter if they were out for five minutes or hours, they knew that a treat and hot chocolate would welcome them back in.

Journaling Space:

TOES

Kneeling next to the bed
Journal is open
Writing about the winter
A long season

Time passes slow
Wind is fast
Fun to be had
Bundled and ready

Hot chocolate or Soup
Movies under blankets
Large Fires
Entertain and warm us

Creating calms me
Writing calms me
Puzzling calms me
Keep creating

Back to thoughts of
This long season
Warm me down to my
Toes

Starting to write in the winter has helped me get through many days that run slowly at home. This poem takes me through all the things that give us joy during the winter.

Journaling Space:

HIBERNATION

I nod in and out
I often rest while in this seat
He laughs
He's the driver

Winter in full force
Dark so soon
Bright fresh snow
Headlights twinkle

Thank you farmers
Sign on the side
Familiar road
Passed over many times

Dead corn stalks
They Peek out
I'm toasty
And snuggly warm

Cold hands
Mittens are kept close
Staying warm
I crave to hibernate

I wrote this on a drive on an evening in Madison. I often sleep when I'm in the passenger seat, but this time I was up and thinking. We passed many things that were familiar as we've driven this road many times. Thinking of how I love to be warm made me think of hibernation and what I sometimes crave in the winter months.

Journaling Space:

BEAUTIFUL

Evening light
The day is on my mind
So is the past
The day closes

Are you tired?
Did you lose weight?
You let them go?
Don't close off

Stay open
Tired of the comments
Lose the judgment
Feel the feels

Find the forgiveness
He forgives
So can I
Let it go

Open.
Stay.
Live the life.
You are beautiful.

Someday, we will all be judged. This helps me reflect on the fact that we are all sinners. It takes me through many times when I was judged. My husband often refers to me as beautiful, which sometimes is hard to hear. Leaning into my faith helps me find forgiveness for others and myself. Judgment exists stronger at times.

Journaling Space:

PAIN

It's been one week
Listen up
I'm still learning
We're still learning
Hustle and bustle
Deadlines approaching
Get it all in
Confusion sets in
Write about it
Document it
Feel it
Breathe it
She doesn't get it
She may feel it
Is it a lie?
Time only knows
Lots can cause it
Many feel it
Who plays the role
When one's in Pain

The poem "Pain" takes me through different people's opinions of me as I'm starting to be creative and open about my creativity. I feel like there will always be someone to judge. I realize now I can't stop it from happening. I just need to be comfortable in my own skin.

Journaling Space:

HEALING

Under my cozy blanket
Gazing towards the river
He rests next to me
We rest together
Ice has formed on the river
The peace it brings
The joy it brings
We love the river
So many gatherings missed
My thoughts
My love
My spirit was present
The check-ins
So much love
So much Caring
Love our Friendships
This pain is leaving
More will come
Through faith and love
All Pain takes Healing

During recovery after a minor surgery, my husband and I both had to slow down. We enjoyed resting and being together. It was very peaceful and quiet. In this quiet time, so many friends and family reached out just to check on me. Our friendships and relationships are strong because we work at them. This is what I needed, to be grateful and forced to slow down during a busy Christmas holiday.

Journaling Space:

SHOES

I step over the pile
I miss the piles
Enjoying them now
Love lives here
They start out small
They Crawl
They Walk
Then they Run
A few pairs at first
As the family grows
So do they
Love grows here
I sit and listen
The giggles
The stories
Love is here
They step away
They step closer
They step back
In their shoes

This poem also comes from our recent gathering as there was a pile of shoes near the door. This was an occurrence at our home when the kids were growing up. It meant they had friends over. It meant there were family gatherings. It meant that there was a party. The shoes represent the different stages of their life. And many more to come.

Journaling Space:

TREE

In the early morning
The moon shines bright
We gathered…
Our leaves shined brighter
Gathering around the table
Their stories were older
They are older
Togetherness
Gathering around the table
Their smiles were bigger
They are bigger
Thoughtfulness
Gathering around the table
Our love is stronger
We are stronger
Tenderness
Time is what we needed
They Light our lives
Brighten our leaves
Our Growing Family Tree

We recently gathered for Christmas together. There was a beautiful tree in our rental property in the evening. The lights in the leaves really brightened up the spot around the table. We gathered there to play games work on puzzles, and to eat our meals. This poem takes me through my kids getting older, bigger, and stronger.

Journaling Space:

To My Yoga Teachers, especially
Pete, Theresa, Lauren, and Ariane

To My Life Coach, Theresa for reminding
me it's alright to…
"Just Be"

ABOUT THE AUTHOR

Emily Howe is a brand-new writer of poetry. When her children began leaving the nest to start their own journeys, Emily found herself searching for her own sense of purpose. During that season, she began meeting with a local life coach with the hope of building a stronger relationship with her ailing father. Over time, that work marked the beginning of a new journey for her.

After her father passed away, Emily experienced a profound moment of enlightenment during a trip to Sedona, Arizona, in March of 2023. She has always believed in signs, and she is certain that her father's spirit has visited her many times. This picture captures one of these moments. When Emily first saw it, she felt an undeniable confirmation—because in that very moment, she had been praying to her father for strength.

Born and raised in Manitowoc, Wisconsin, Emily and her husband Mike chose to raise their four children there. When she's not writing poetry, Emily enjoys spending time with family and friends in cozy coffee shops, gathering around large bonfires, and going to concerts.

www.ingramcontent.com/pod-product-compliance
Lightning Source LLC
LaVergne TN
LVHW010614100826
845148LV00014B/2965

* 9 7 8 1 6 8 4 8 8 1 8 9 5 *